LEARN ABOUT VALUES

COURAGE

by Cynthia A. Klingel

Published in the United States of America by The Child's World®
1980 Lookout Drive • Mankato, MN 56003-1705 • 800-599-READ • www.childsworld.com

The Child's World®: Mary Berendes, Publishing Director; Katherine Stevenson, Editor
The Design Lab: Kathy Petelinsek, Art Director; Julia Goozen, Design and Page Production

Photo Credits: © Brand X Pictures: 11; © David M. Budd Photography: 7, 9, 15, 17; © image100/Corbis: 5; © Randy Faris/Corbis: 21; © Stéphane Rochon/Alamy: 19; © Tom & Dee Ann McCarthy/Corbis: 13; © Wolf/zefa/Corbis: cover

Library of Congress Cataloging-in-Publication Data
Klingel, Cynthia Fitterer.
  Courage / by Cynthia A. Klingel.
    p. cm. — (Learn about values)
  ISBN 978-1-59296-667-7 ISBN 1-59296-667-5 (library bound: alk. paper)
  1. Courage—Juvenile literature. 2. Values—Juvenile literature. I. Title. II. Series.
  BJ1533.C8K55 2006
  179'.6—dc22   2006000937

CONTENTS

What Is Courage?

There are many scary things in life. Maybe you are scared to climb the big slide at the park. Maybe you are afraid of the dark. Courage is having the strength to beat your fears. Courage is being brave!

Showing courage makes you feel good!

Courage at School

It takes courage to stand up to your classmates! Imagine that you are taking a test. Your friend wants to **copy** your answers. You are scared to say no. You are afraid your friend will not like you anymore. You show courage by saying no—and by telling your friend it is wrong to copy.

It can take courage to stand up to a friend.

Making New Friends

It takes courage to make new friends! Maybe you see a new student eating alone at lunchtime. You might be scared to talk to him. You show courage by sitting with him and talking to him. Your courage can help you make more friends!

It can take courage to talk to someone new.

Learning New Sports

It takes courage to learn new things! You might be afraid to try something new. Maybe there is a sport you are scared to try. You are afraid you might get hurt or look silly. You show courage by trying the sport. Maybe you will like it and have fun!

Having the courage to try something new feels good!

11

Putting on a Show

It takes courage to do things in front of people! Maybe your piano teacher is having a **recital**. You might be scared to play in front of people. You think people will laugh if you play poorly. You show courage by going on stage and doing your best.

Playing in front of other people takes courage.

Saying "I'm Sorry"

It takes courage to say "I'm sorry" after a fight! Maybe you and a friend had a big fight. You said mean things to your friend. Your friend said things that hurt your feelings, too. You are scared to be the first one to **apologize**. You show courage by calling your friend and making up.

It takes courage to say that you were wrong.

Being Responsible

It takes courage to be **responsible**! Imagine that you and your brother are wrestling. Your knock over and break your mother's special vase. You might be scared to tell your mother what happened. You are afraid she will be angry. You are afraid you will get into trouble. You show courage by telling your mother—even if it means you might be **punished**.

It takes courage to be honest about your mistakes.

Doing Something Scary

It takes courage to do something scary! Maybe you are afraid to swim. You do not like to put your head underwater. You show courage by taking swimming lessons. Maybe you will like swimming after all!

Many things that seem scary turn out to be fun!

19

Courage Makes You Stronger

Showing courage can be hard! It means doing something that is a little scary. But showing courage helps you test yourself. It helps you learn new things. Courage helps you grow and makes you feel good!

Showing courage helps you grow up!

glossary

apologize
When you apologize, you say "I'm sorry."

copy
When you copy something, you do it exactly as it is done somewhere else.

punished
Being punished is getting in trouble for doing something bad.

recital
In a recital, you play music in front of other people.

responsible
Being responsible means being able to choose between right and wrong.

books

Hirschmann, Kris. *Courage.* Austin, TX: Raintree, 2003.

Maier, Inger. *When Lizzy Was Afraid of Trying New Things.* Washington, DC: Magination Press, 2004.

Sperry, Armstrong. *Call It Courage.* New York: Aladdin, 1990.

web sites

Visit our Web page for links about character education and values:
http://www.childsworld.com/links

Note to parents, teachers, and librarians:
We routinely check our Web links to make sure they're safe,
active sites—so encourage your readers to check them out!

index

about the author

Cynthia A. Klingel is Director of Curriculum and Instruction for a school district in Minnesota. She enjoys reading, writing, gardening, traveling, and spending time with friends and family.